BLACK BEAR CUB

SMITHSONIAN
WILD HERITAGE COLLECTION

To Anita, Deborah, and Lisa,
the ladies who made this book possible.
— A. L.

To Morgan
— K. L.

Copyright © 1994 by Trudy Management Corporation,
165 Water Street, Norwalk, CT 06856, and the Smithsonian Institution,
Washington, DC 20560.

Book Design: Johanna P. Shields

10 9 8 7 6 5 4 3
Printed in Singapore

Library of Congress Cataloging-in-Publication Data

Lind, Alan.

Black Bear Cub / by Alan Lind ;
illustrated by Katie Lee.
         p.   cm.
Summary: After hibernating all winter, Mother Bear takes Black Bear Cub and his
sister out of their den and teaches them how to survive in the forest.
        ISBN 1-56899-030-8
1. Bears — Juvenile fiction. [1. Bears — Fiction. 2. Animals — Infancy — Fiction.]
I. Lee, Katie, ill. II. Title.
        PZ10.3.L6355Bl 1994   93-31130
        (E) — dc20   CIP
                                                     AC

BLACK BEAR CUB

by Alan Lind
Illustrated by Katie Lee

A Division of Trudy Management Corporation
Norwalk, Connecticut

In early spring, Mother Bear and her two cubs lumber out of their winter den. Black Bear Cub slips and tumbles in a slushy mound of snow and lets out a wail. Mother Bear picks up Bear Cub gently with her mouth. She carries him slowly to the edge of a small stream, where she sets him next to his sister.

Mother Bear reaches her head down and takes a long drink of water. She has spent the winter sleeping and has had no food or water for months. Still drowsy from her long sleep, Mother Bear leads Bear Cub and his sister back to the den. They curl up and sleep for a few more days.

When the first green leaves appear on the forest trees, Mother Bear and her cubs leave the den again. Food is still scarce on the forest floor. But the tender new leaves lure Mother Bear to climb an aspen tree.

Bear Cub and his sister both try to climb after her. Their claws are already sharp, but, halfway up, Bear Cub loses his grip and falls to the ground with a thump. His sister decides she has climbed high enough for this day, and she climbs down to join him. The cubs will practice climbing again tomorrow.

In a few days the cubs are expert climbers. Mother Bear can leave them on their own for a little while. She goes off to forage on the early green shoots of buttercups and the leaves of violets and wild strawberries. The cubs remain behind, beneath the low-hanging branches of a pine tree in a nest of dry pine needles. If they sense any danger, they will quickly climb the tree.

When the summer days grow warmer, Bear Cub splashes through a cool, shallow stream. He rushes to catch up with his sister. Ahead of them both, Mother Bear plods steadily through the water.

When the stream widens into a pool, Mother Bear lies down to let the water cool her. Bear Cub and his sister sit on the mossy stream bank and wait.

As Mother Bear leaves the pool, she stands upright, sniffing the air, testing it for danger. The cubs stand up, too. They try to sniff the air just the way their mother does it. Like all black bears, their eyesight is poor, and their noses tell them far more than their eyes.

All is well.

Mother Bear leads the cubs to a dead oak tree. She hears a swarm of honey bees buzzing around a large hole in the tree. The cubs wait as she climbs the tree and claws at the hole until pieces of wood break off and fall to the ground.

The bees get angry and try to sting her, but her fur is too thick. Whenever she has a chance, she licks a mouthful of bees from her fur and swallows them. They make a tasty snack.

When Mother Bear rips away enough of the rotted tree to uncover the bee hive, she takes a big piece of honeycomb for herself. Then she drops chunks down to the cubs. Bear Cub and his sister sit on the ground, munching greedily at the thick, sweet honey. Their fur soon becomes sticky, and they lick themselves clean with their long, pink tongues. Bear Cub's tongue is so long he can almost lick between his eyes.

Tired and full from the sweet honey, Mother Bear lies, cooling herself in the shade of a pine tree at the edge of a small clearing. Nearby, Bear Cub climbs a twelve-foot aspen tree just for the fun of it. As he climbs, the tree bends with his weight. When he nears the top, the bending tree swings him gently to the ground. Bear Cub and his sister ride the aspen trees over and over again.

After a while, Bear Cub leaves his sister and bounds to his mother's side. He pulls himself onto his mother's back and playfully bites at her ears. She pays no attention to him as he climbs across her back and shoulders.

Suddenly, Mother Bear rises, surprising Bear Cub and flipping him to the ground. She rushes into the clearing, then turns to bark at the cubs. They understand her command and run to the nearest large tree, where they climb to the safety of the highest branches.

On the far side of the clearing, three coyotes bound from the forest. Protecting her cubs, Mother Bear springs forward, growling. Her head down and teeth bared, she challenges the coyotes. They stop for a moment and pace back and forth. While they decide what to do, Mother Bear rushes to the tree and joins her cubs in the high branches.

28

As the coyotes circle about the tree trunk, yipping and growling, the bears make themselves comfortable. Resting in the high branches, they ignore the coyotes until they give up and leave the clearing.

The bears spend the night in the tree to be certain the coyotes are really gone. In the early morning light, Mother Bear climbs down. Then she woofs her permission for the cubs to join her on the ground. Together they will go in search of a patch of berries.

Bear Cub and his sister will spend the rest of the summer with their mother, while she teaches them all they need to know to survive in the forest. During the cool weather of autumn, they will find another snug den and fill it with grass and leaves. There they will sleep through the winter. When spring finally comes, Bear Cub and his sister will be ready to begin their own lives in the forest.

About the Black Bear

Black bears live in wooded areas of North America from Alaska and Canada to northern Mexico and Florida. Black bears vary in color. Most are black, others are various shades of brown, and there is even a small group whose fur is pale blue bordering on white. Black bears are not an endangered species, but they are threatened by the destruction of the forests in which they live. They will rarely, if ever, attack a large animal or a human. They feed mostly on vegetation, nuts, and fruit.

Glossary

aspen: a hardwood tree that grows in sunny areas across most of North America. Its leaves and stems are flat and flutter in the slightest breeze. The aspen's range begins in Canada. In the east, it extends as far south as Virginia, and, in the west, as far south as Mexico.

bank: the edge of a river, stream, pond, road, path or steep hill.

den: the home of an animal, often in a cave or hole in the ground. Black bears like to make their dens in holes under the roots of large overturned trees.

forest: a thick growth of trees and other plants that covers a considerable area.

moss: very small green plants that grow in patches on the ground, rocks and tree trunks.

pool: a small body of still water.

stream: running water that moves in a path downhill across land. The term stream usually refers to a small river or creek.

Points of Interest in this Book

pp. 4-5 cardinal.

pp. 4-5, 24-25, 26-27 mountain laurel.

pp. 8-9 robin.

pp. 10-11 littlewood satyr (butterfly), ladyslipper orchid, trout lily.

pp. 10-11, 14-15, 16-17, 18-19, 24-25 honey bees.

pp. 10-11, 12-13 wild strawberries.

pp. 10-11, 14-15 fiddleleaf fern.

pp. 12-13 painted turtles, blue flag iris, forget-me-not, dragonfly.

pp. 14-15 clustered psathyrella (mushroom), hairy woodpecker.

pp. 20-21 ladybird.

pp. 20-21, 22-23 tiger swallowtail (butterfly).

pp. 20-21, 24-25, 26-27 Queen Ann's Lace.

pp. 22-23 ants, golden trumpet mushroom.

pp. 24-25 woodfrog, mockingbird.

pp. 24-25, 26-27 coyote tracks.

pp. 26-27 blackberry bush.

pp. 30-31 deer mice, rose hips, bittersweet, ferns, grapevine.

Winfield Public School
OS150 Park Street
Winfield, IL 60190